Floral SHADING

A Grayscale Coloring Book

COLORING BOOK FOR ADULTS

COLOR TEST PAGE

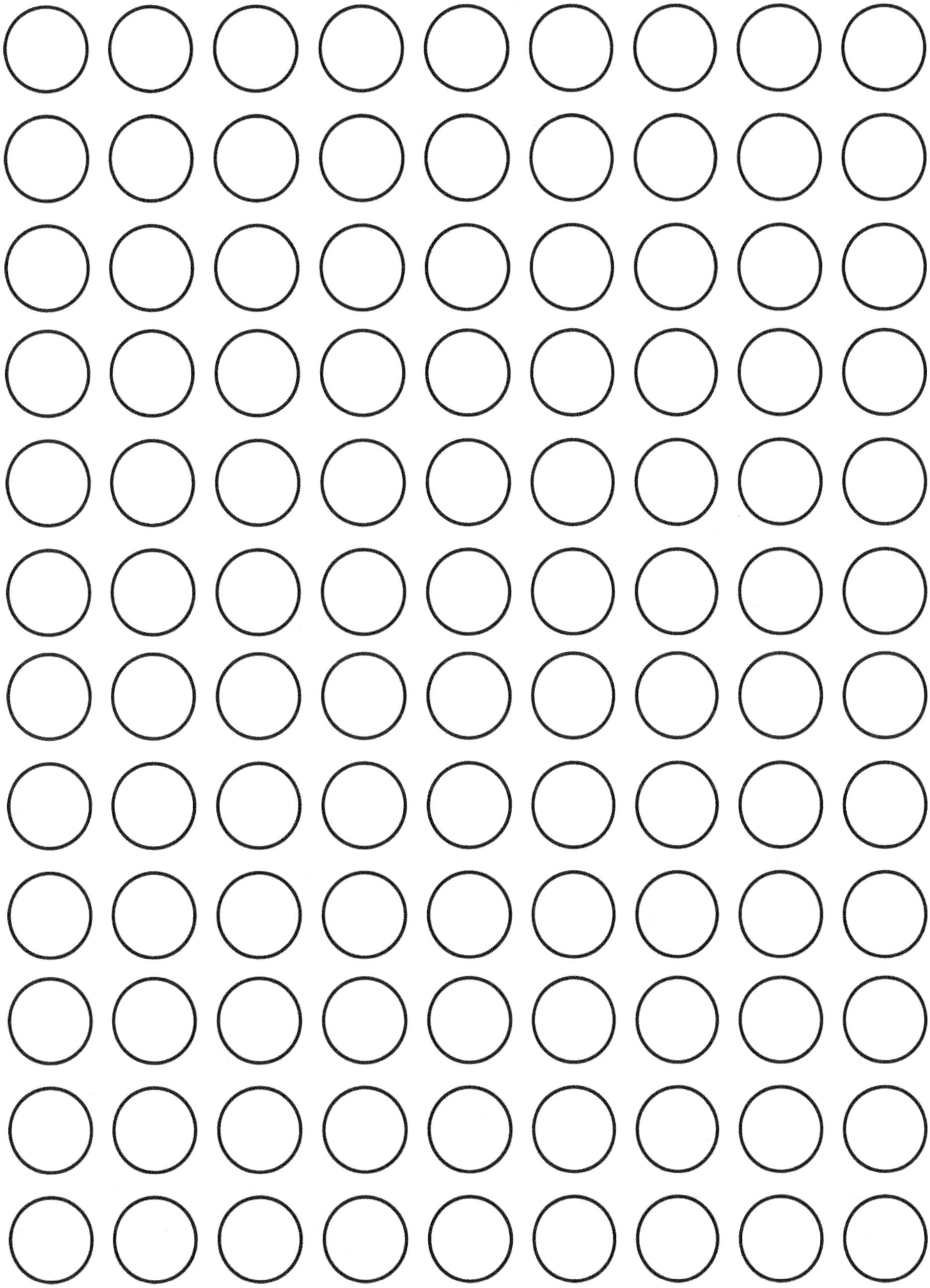

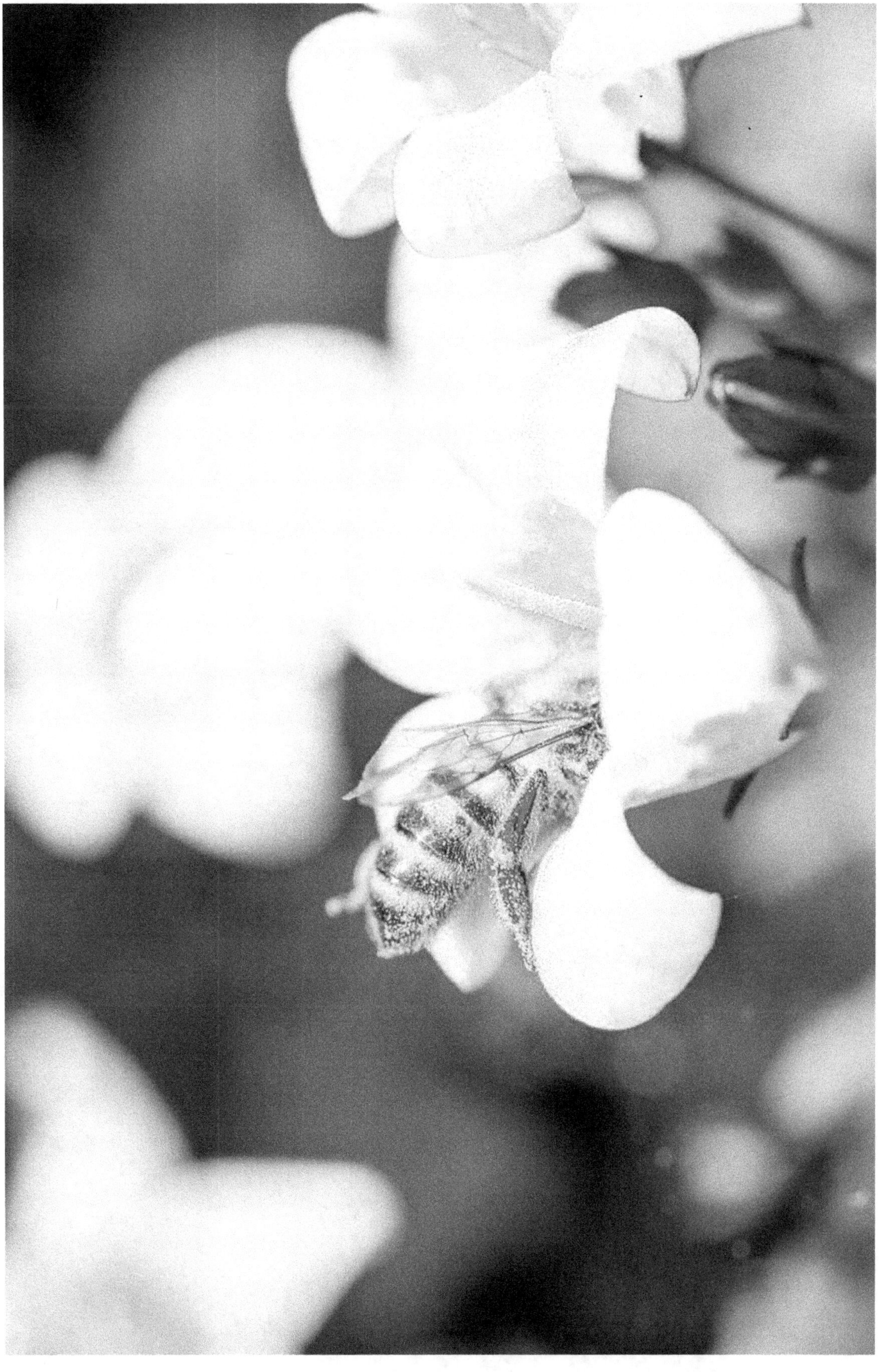

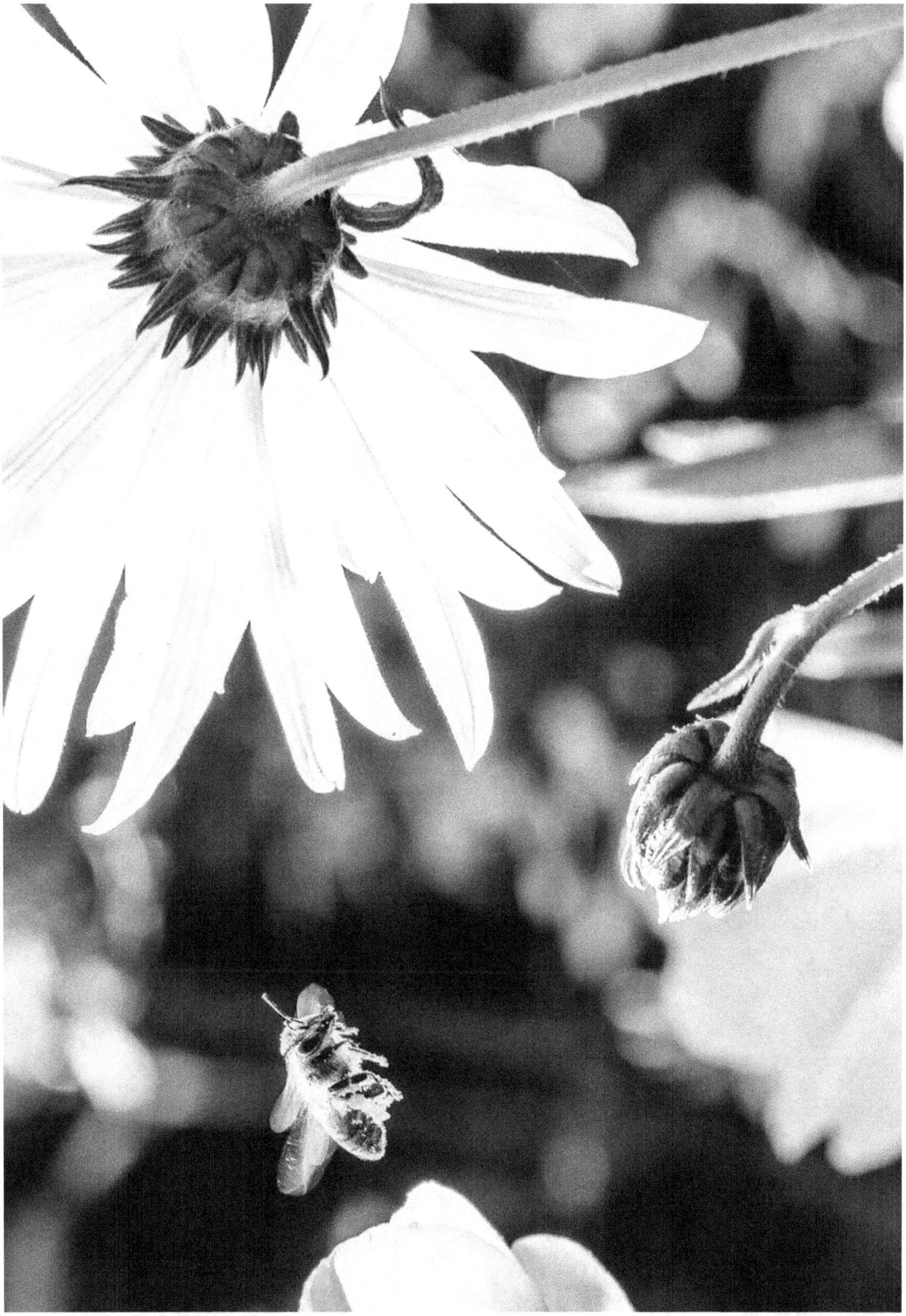

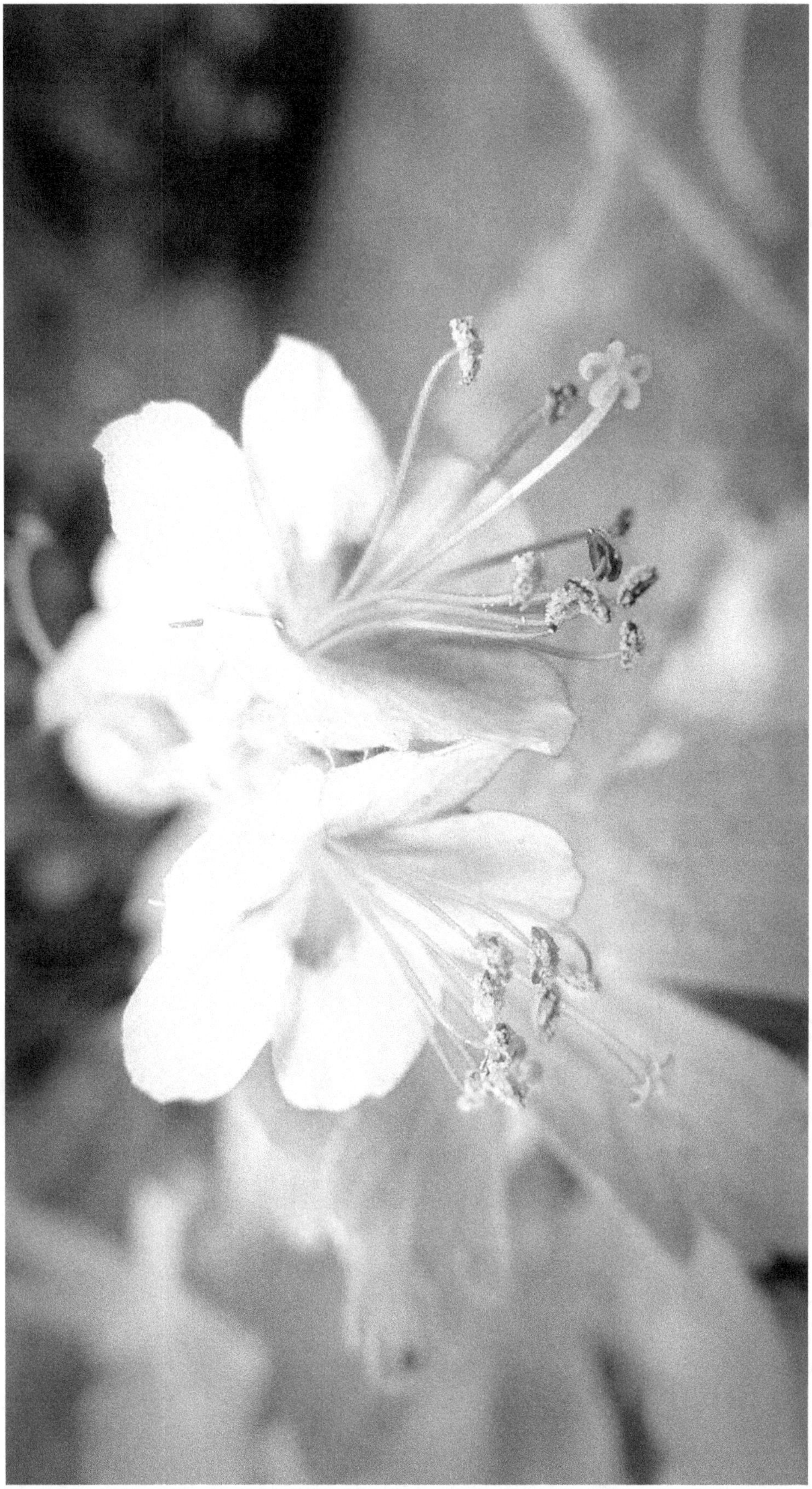

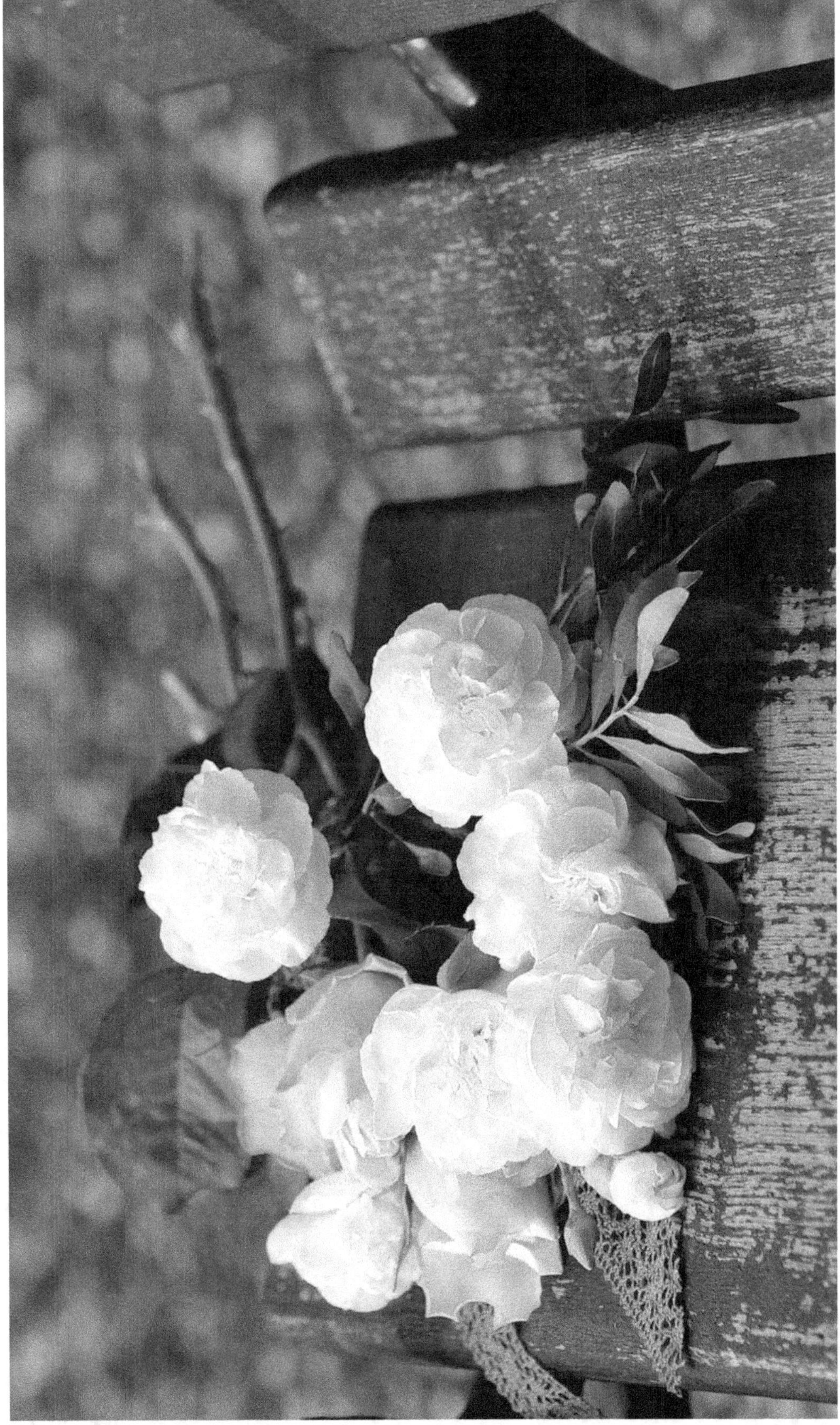

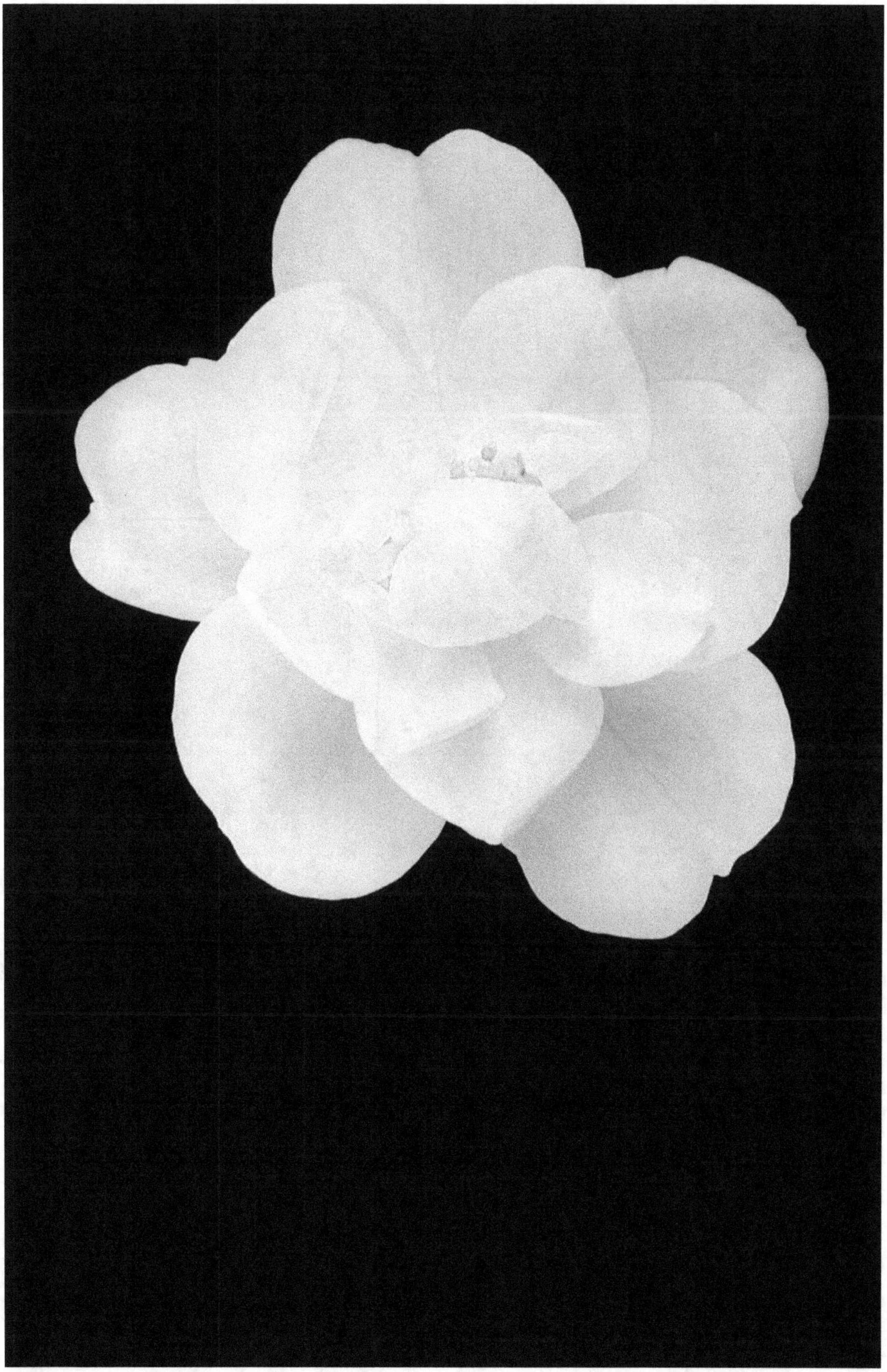

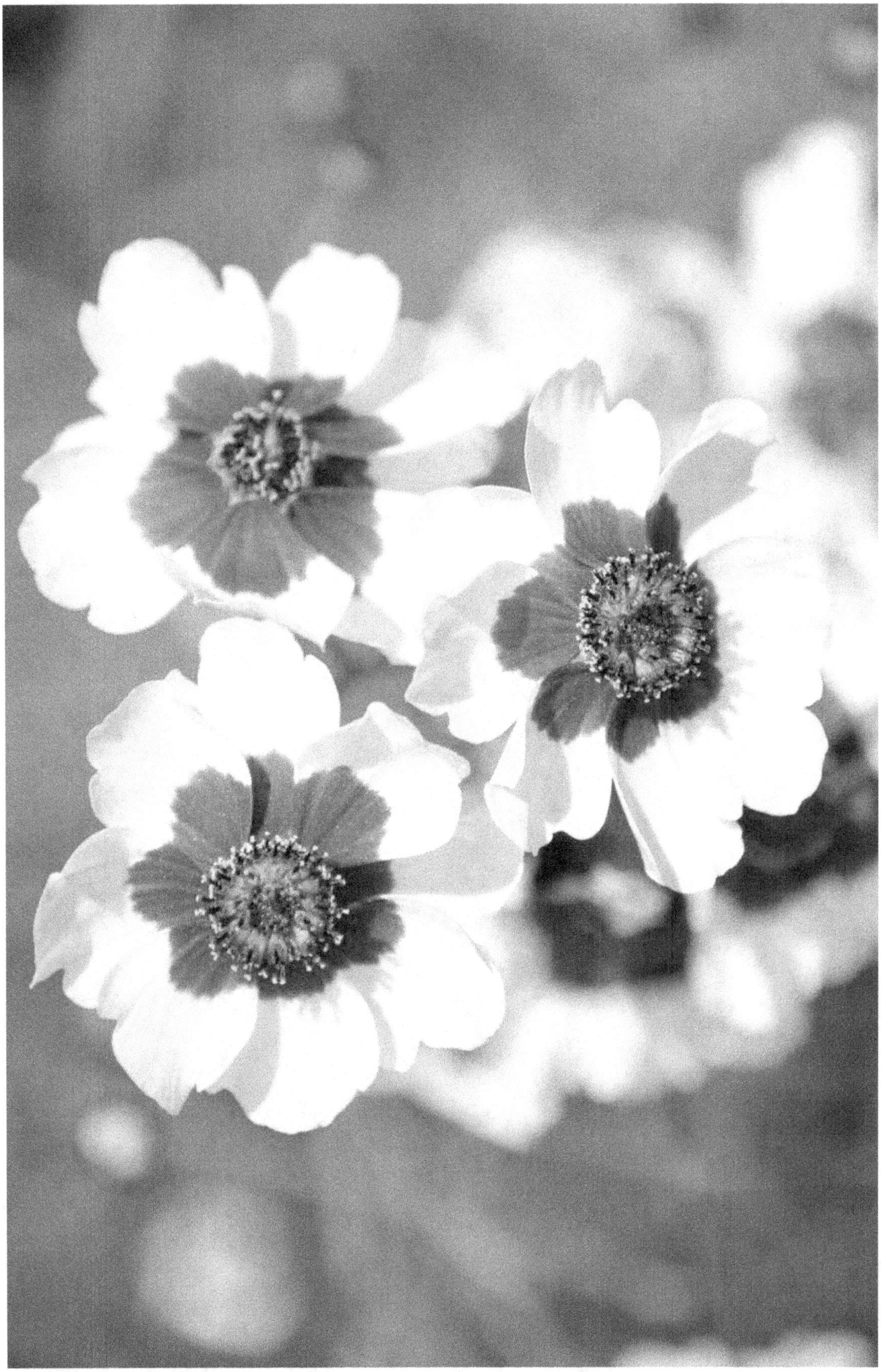

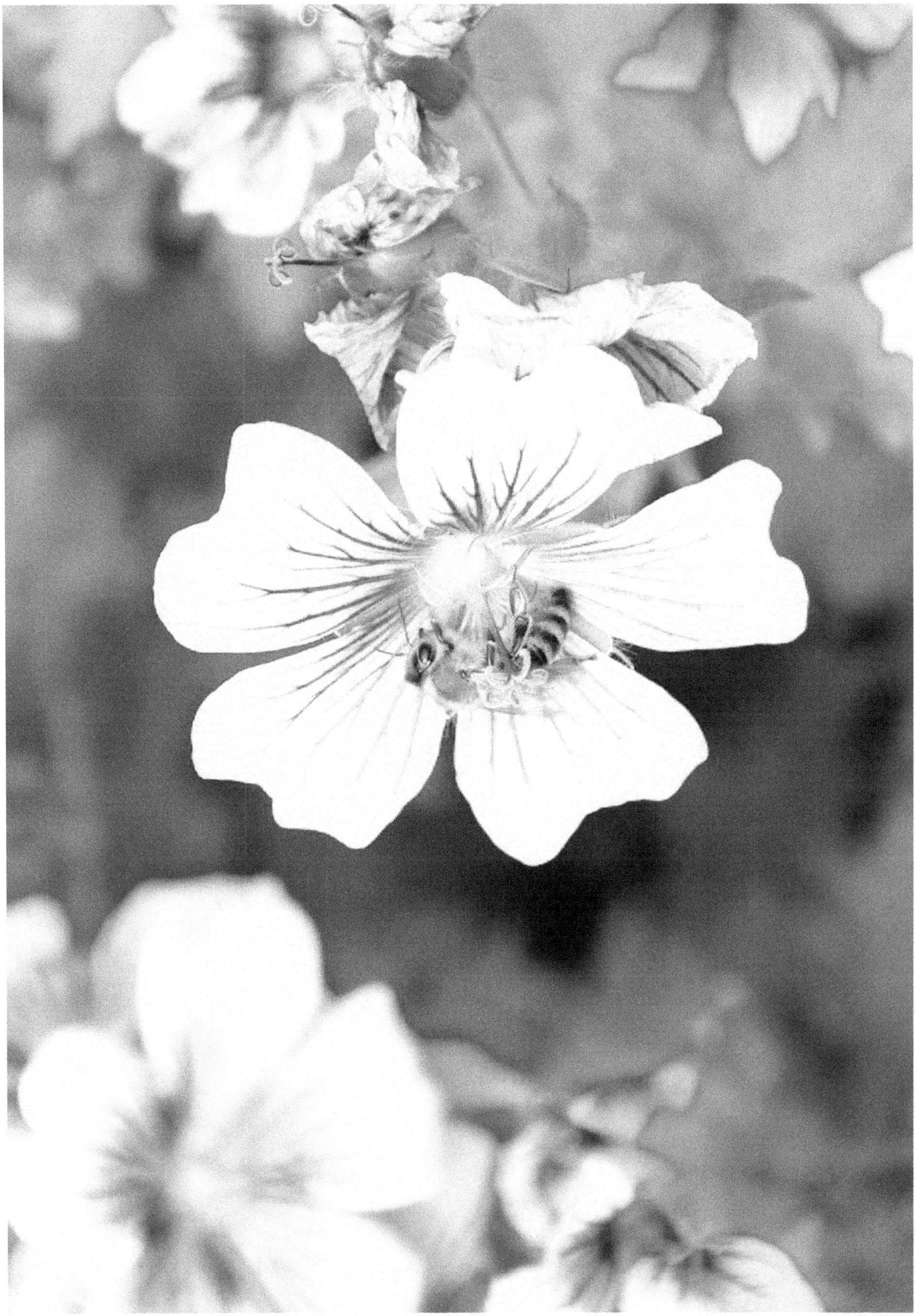

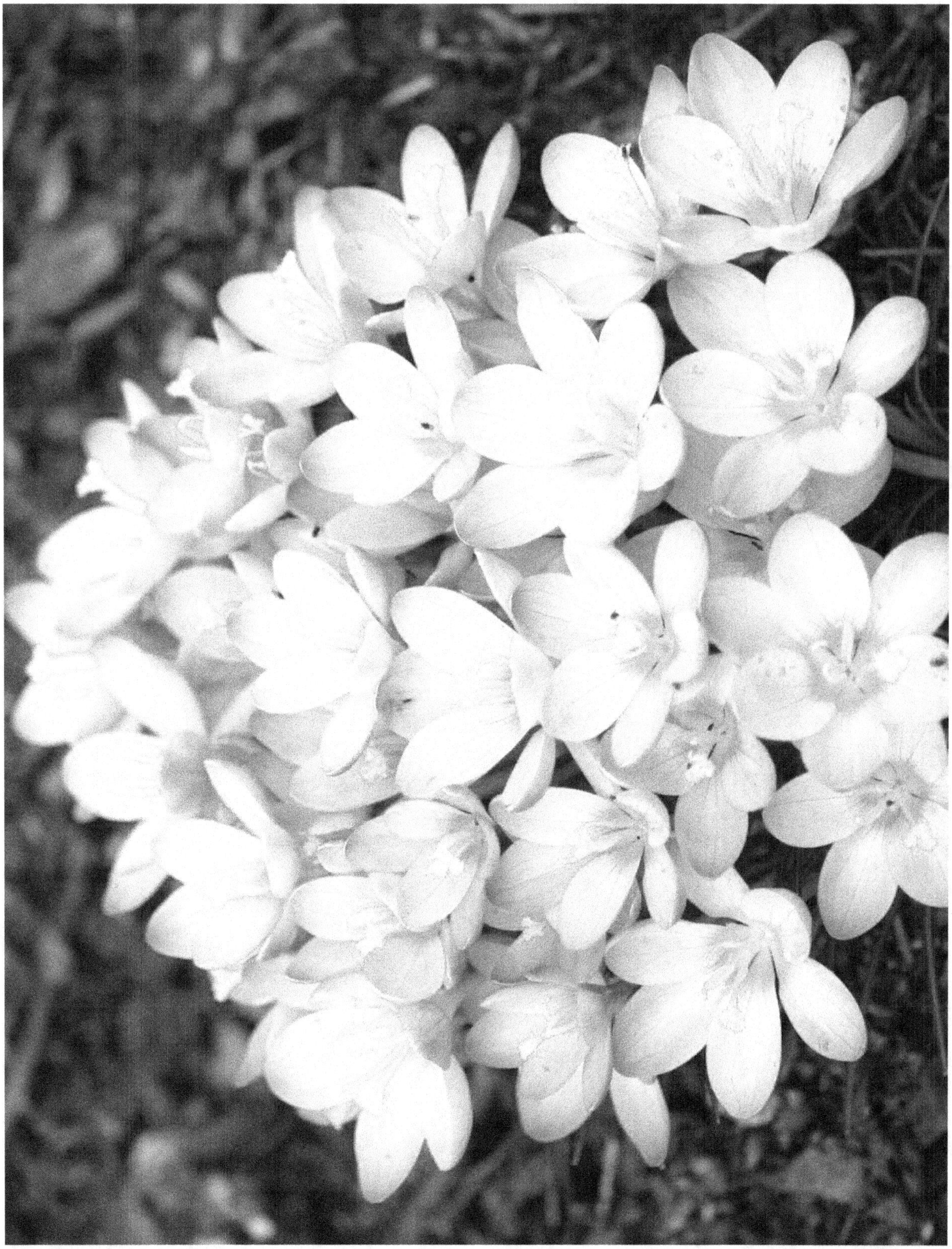

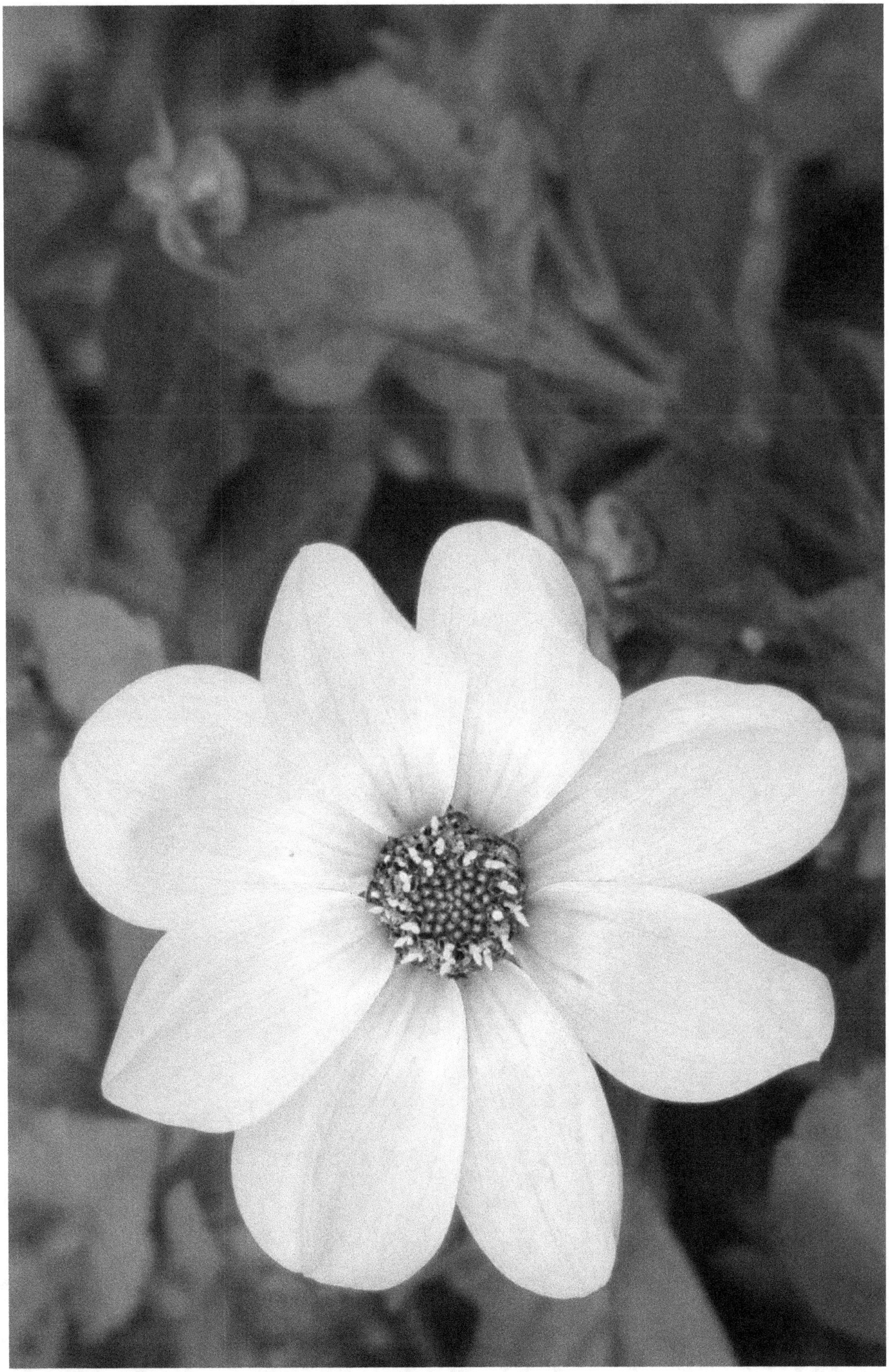

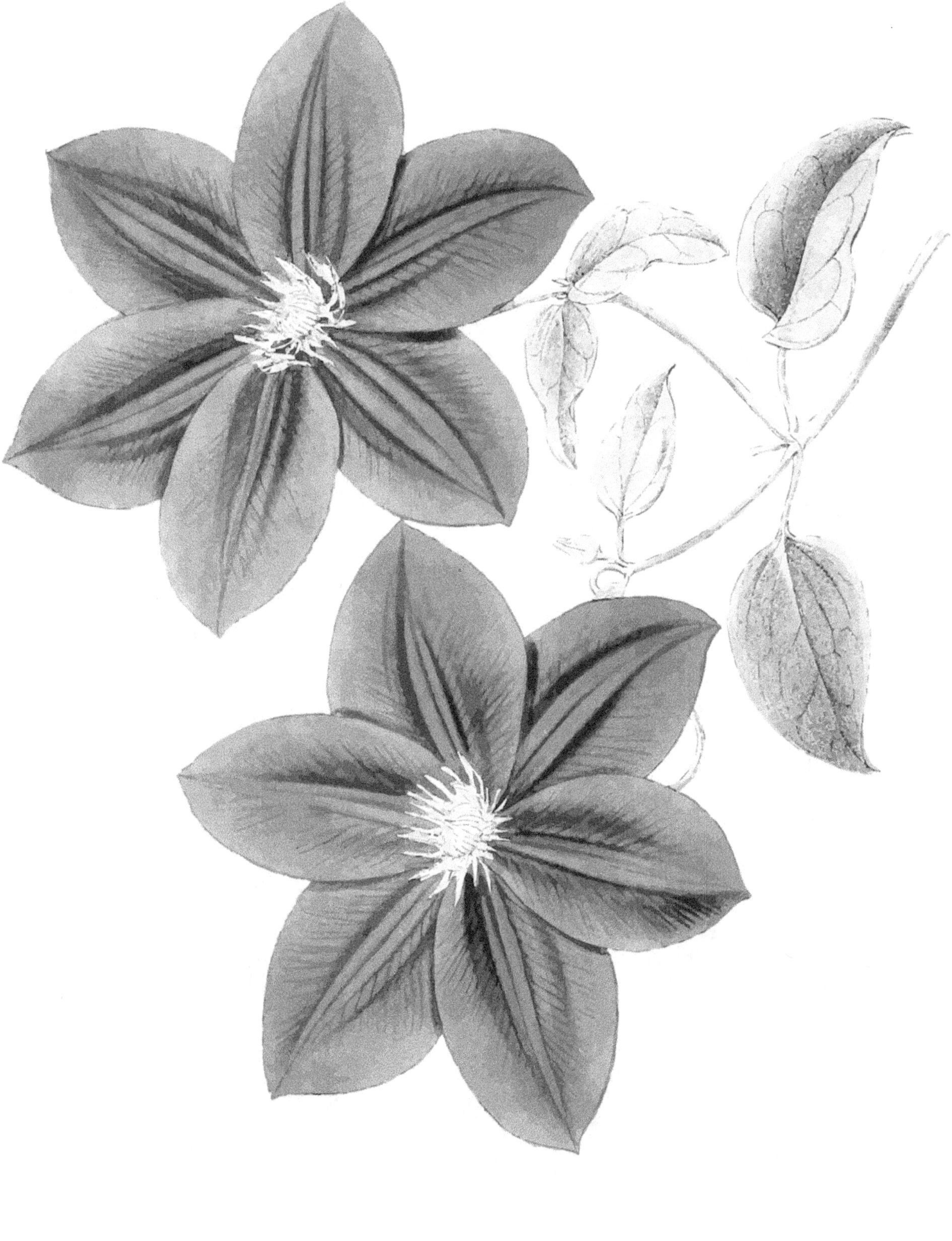

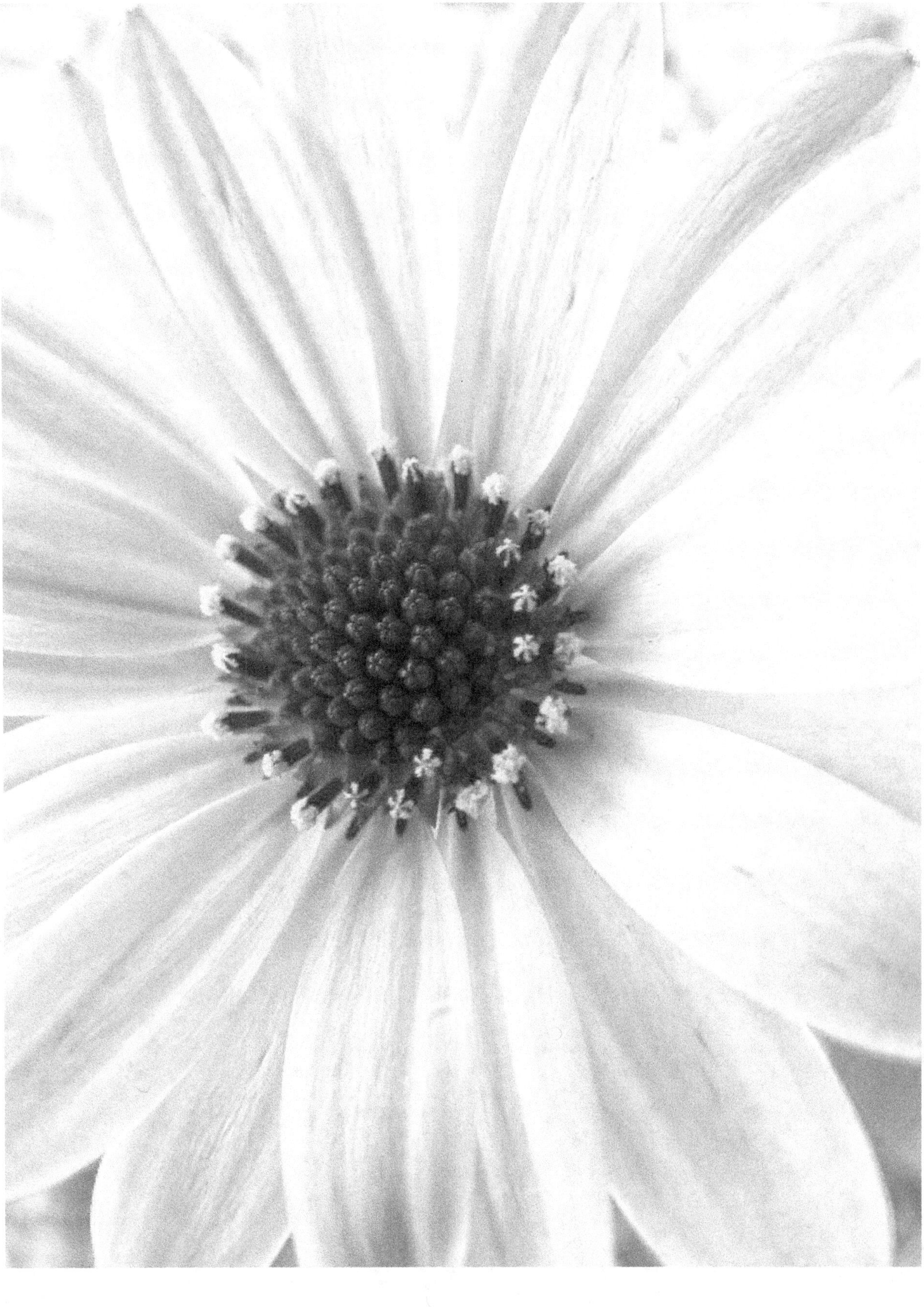

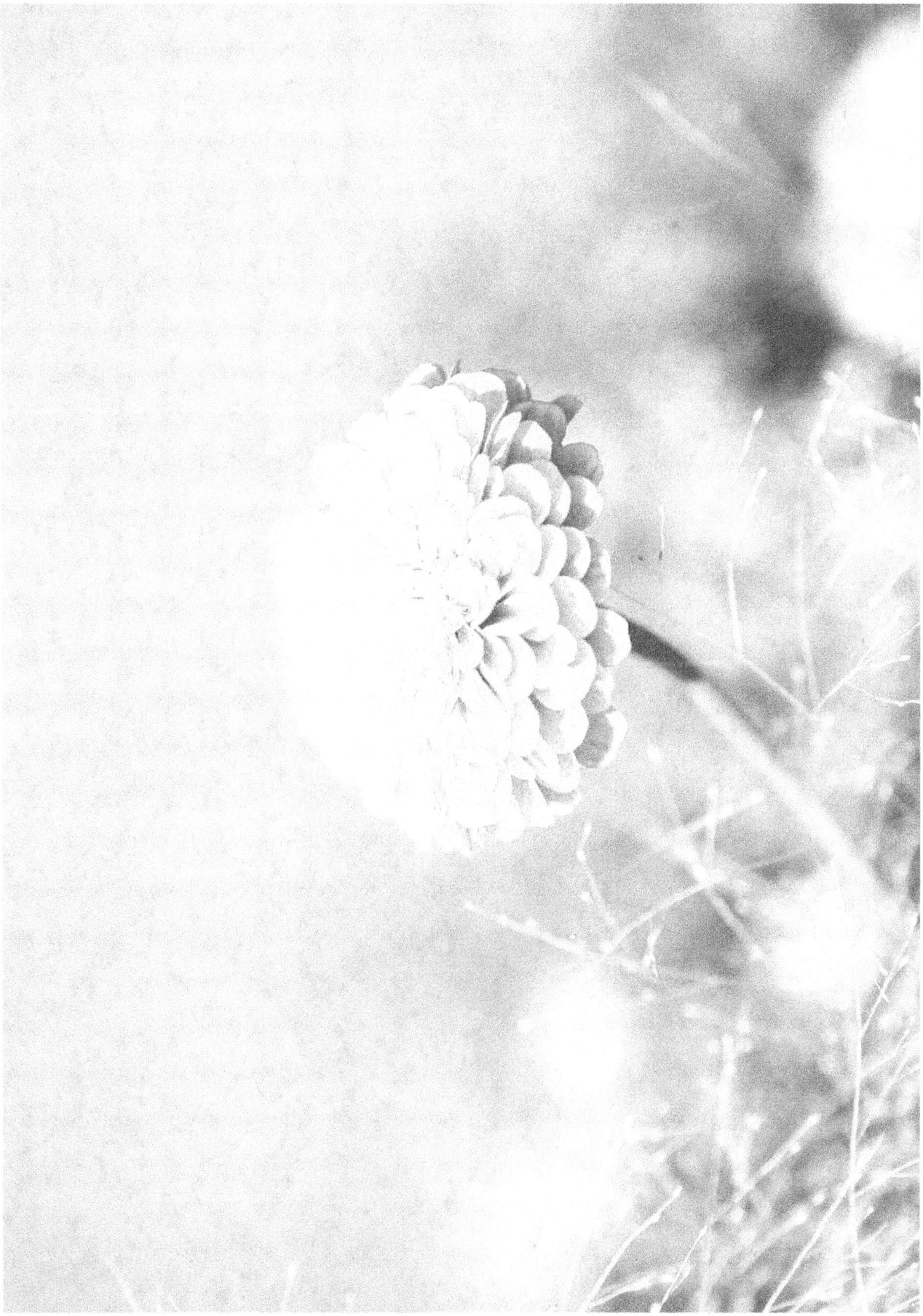

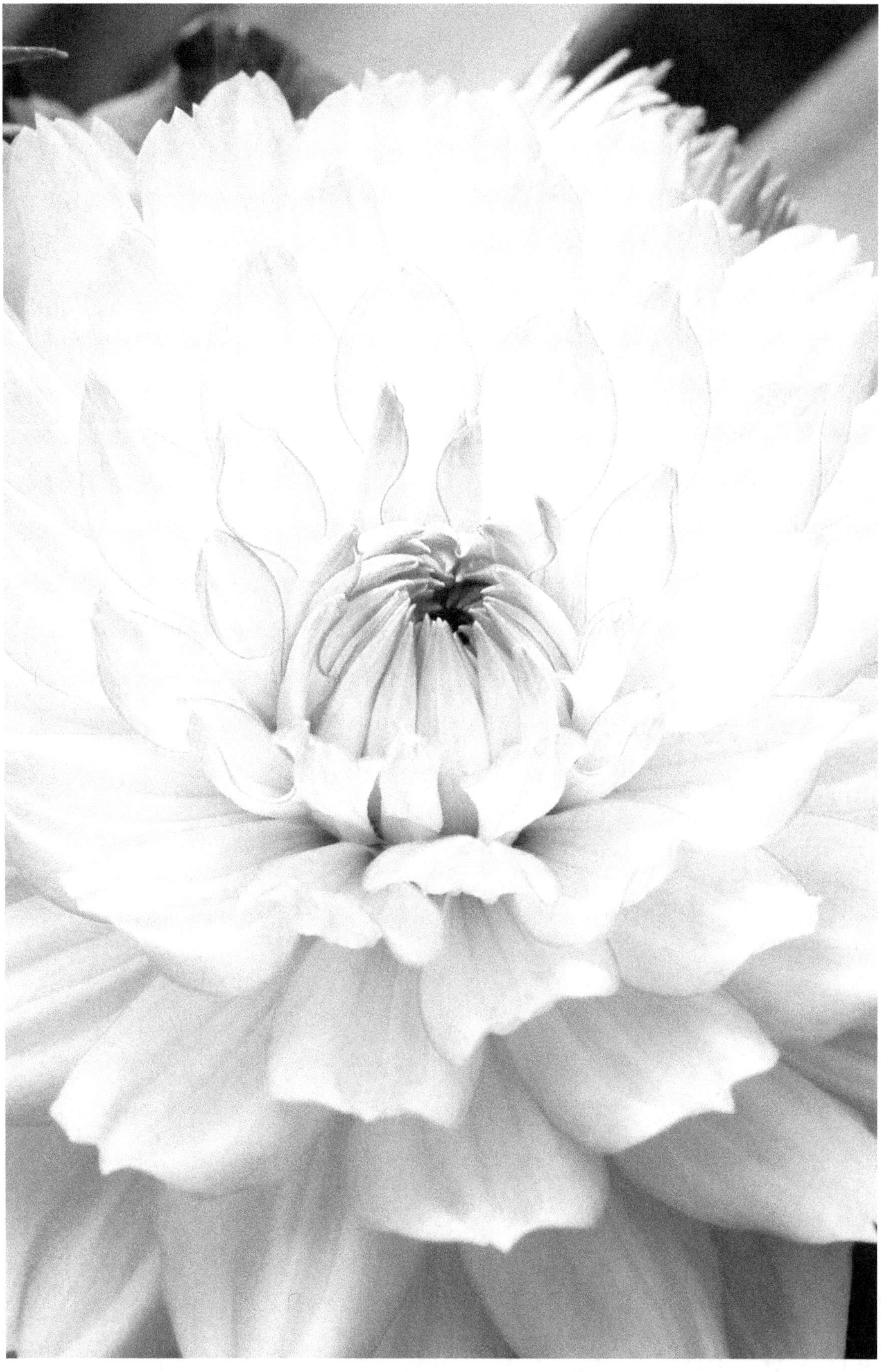

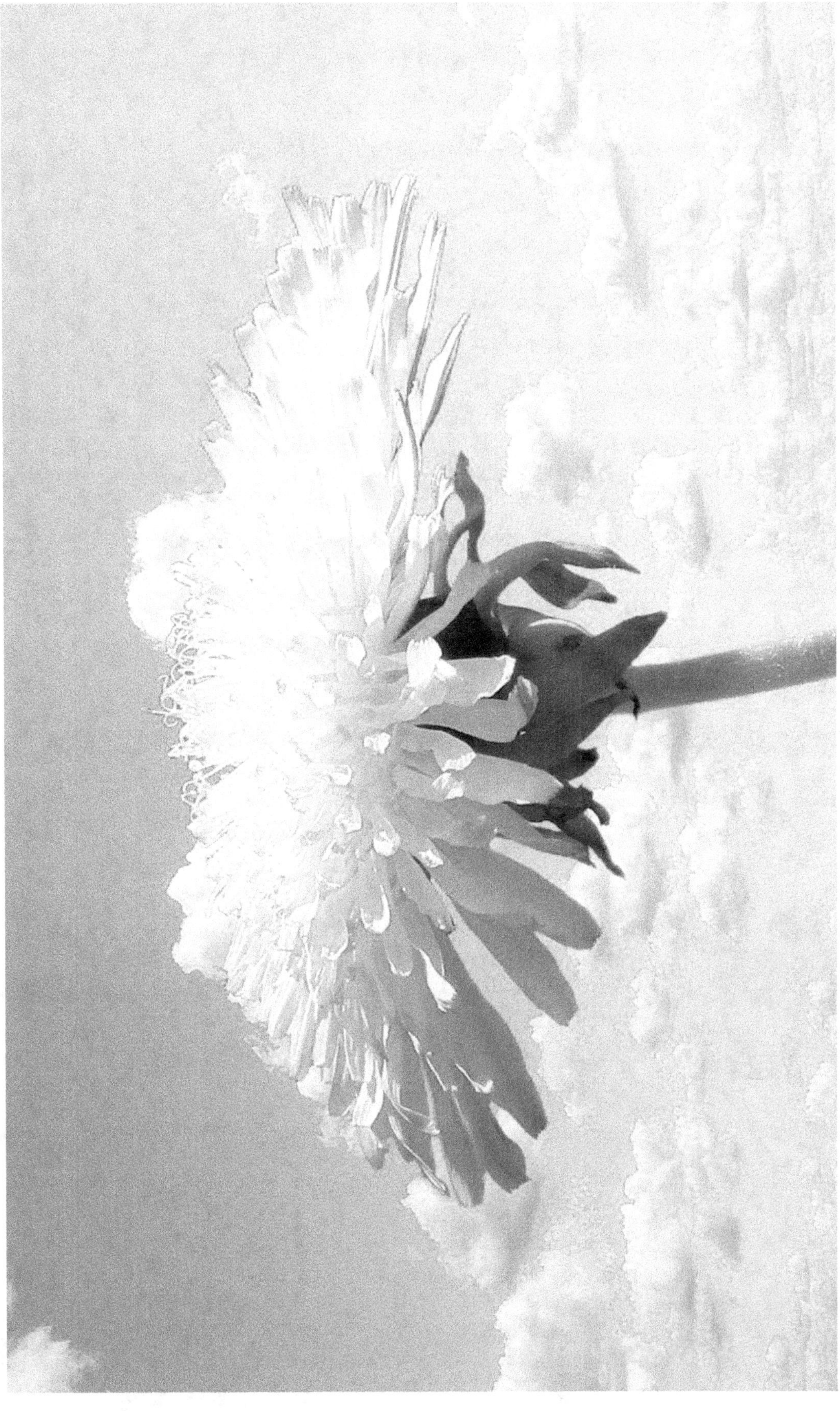

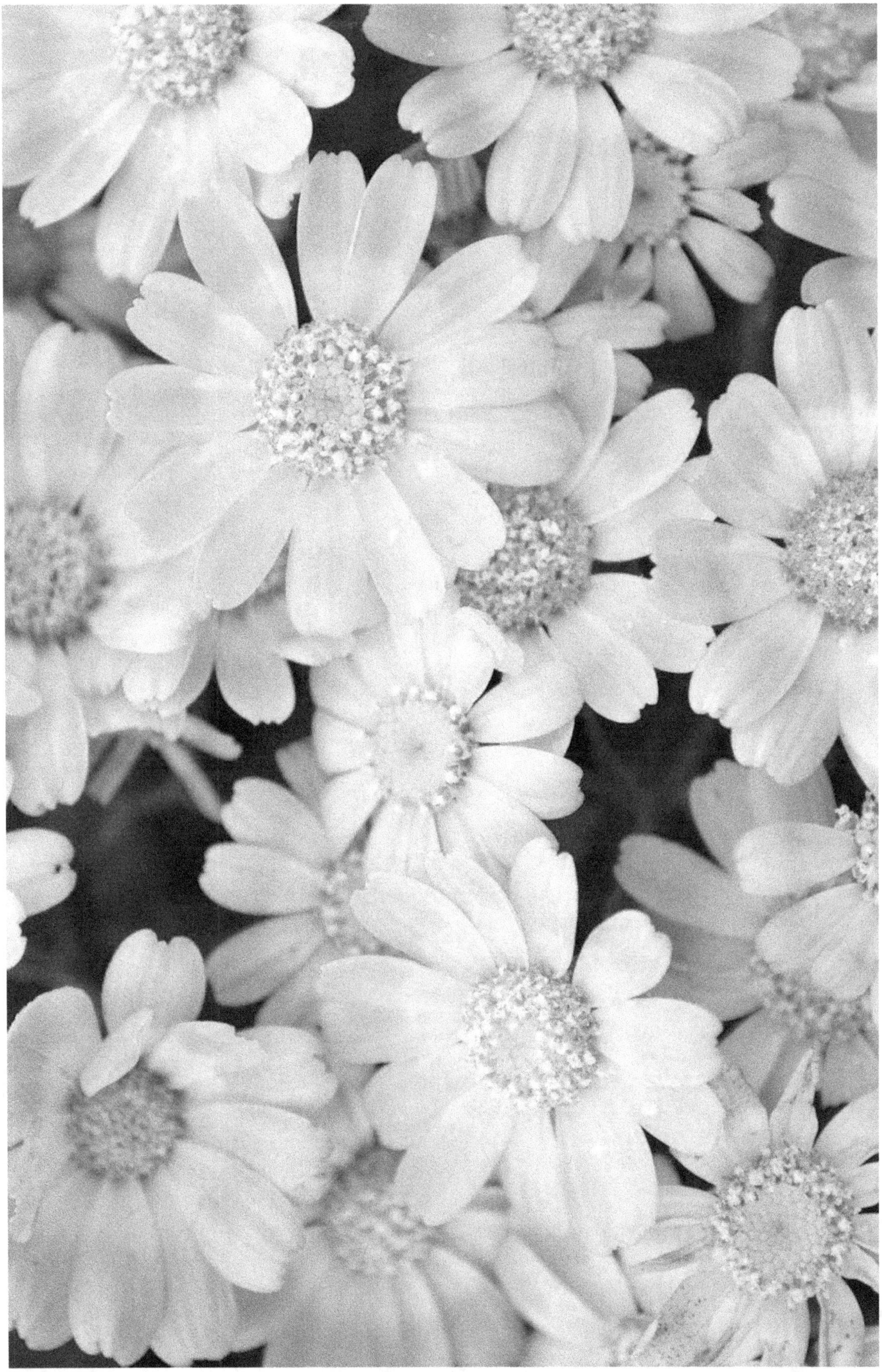

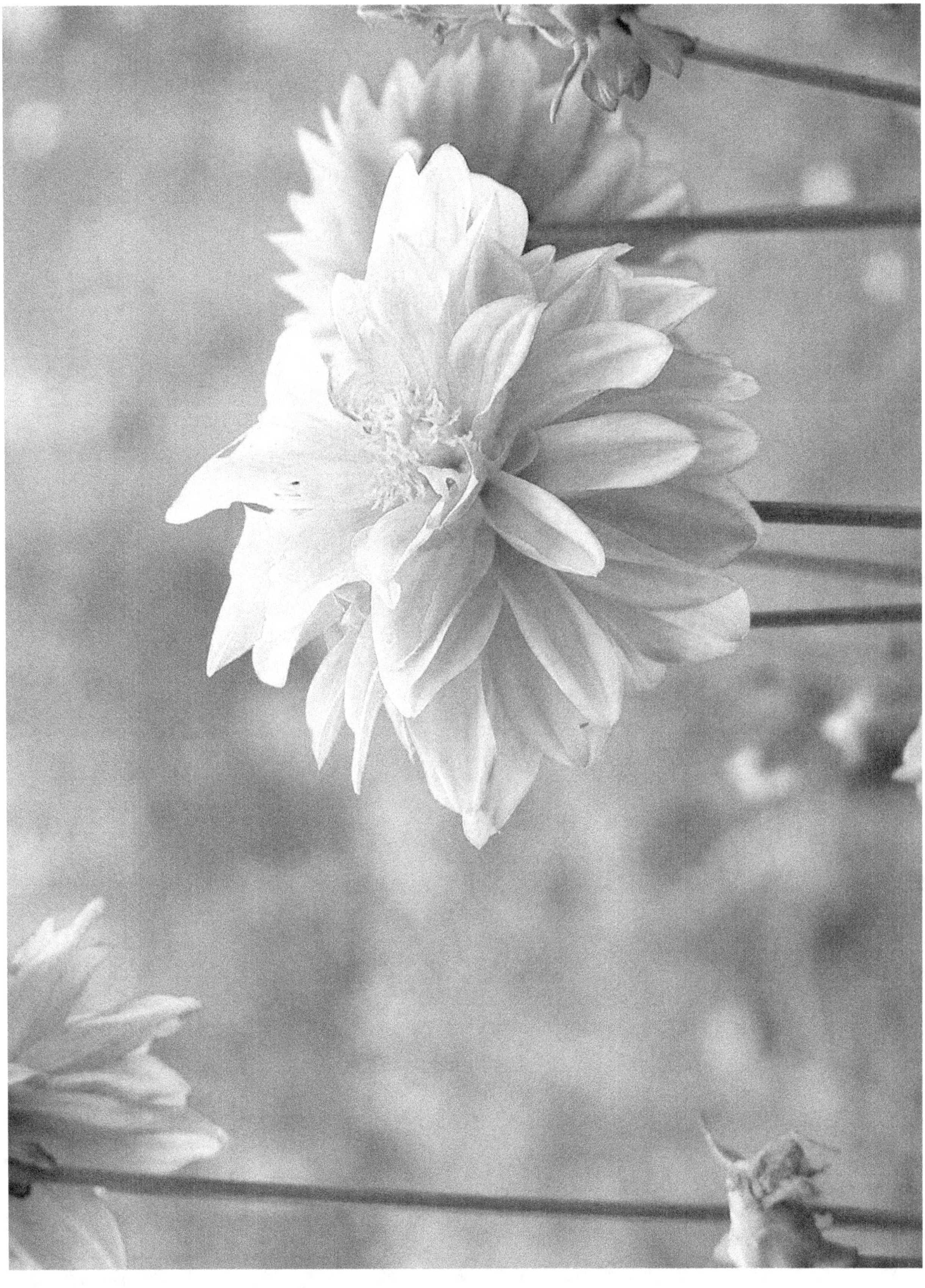

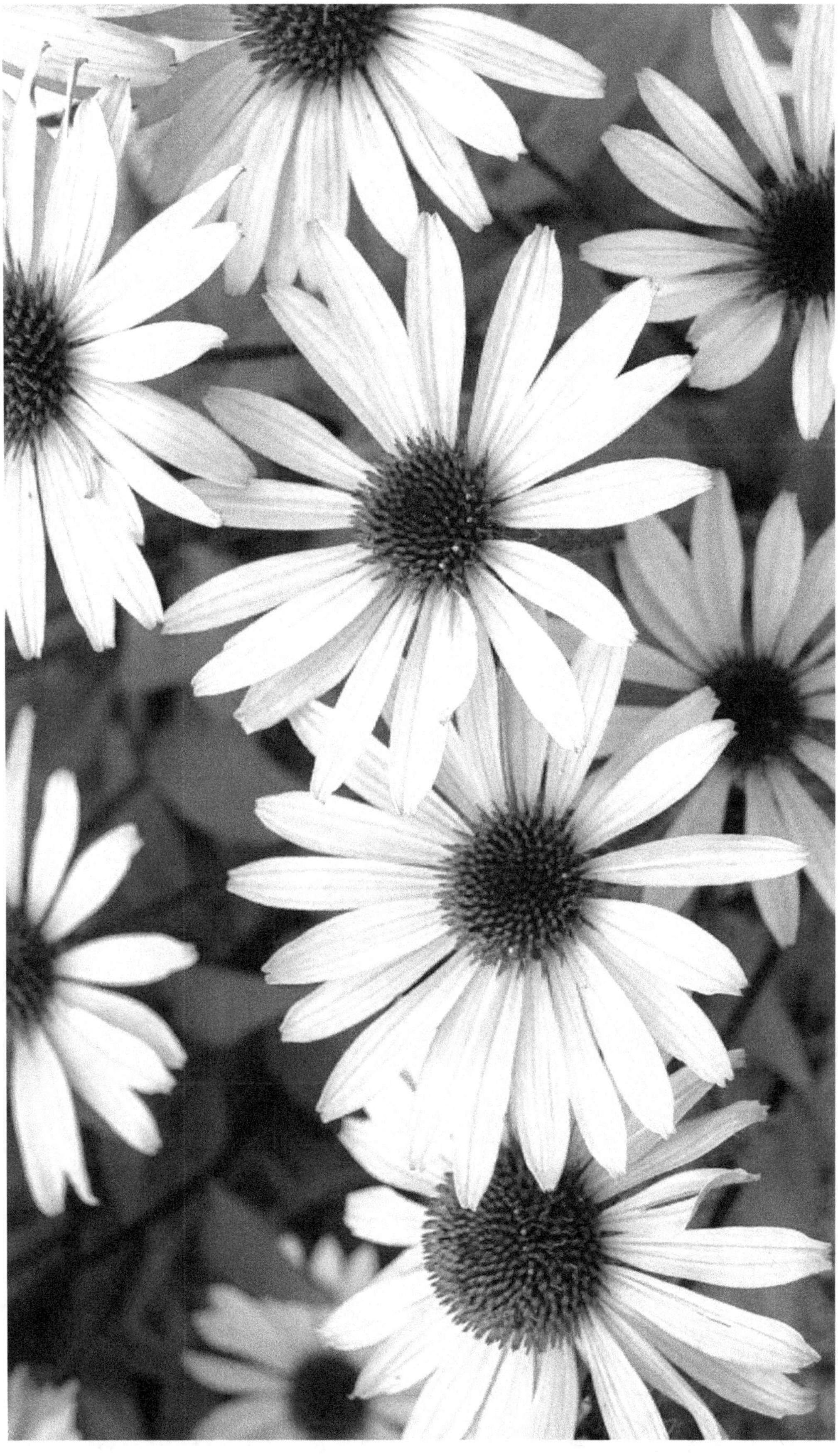

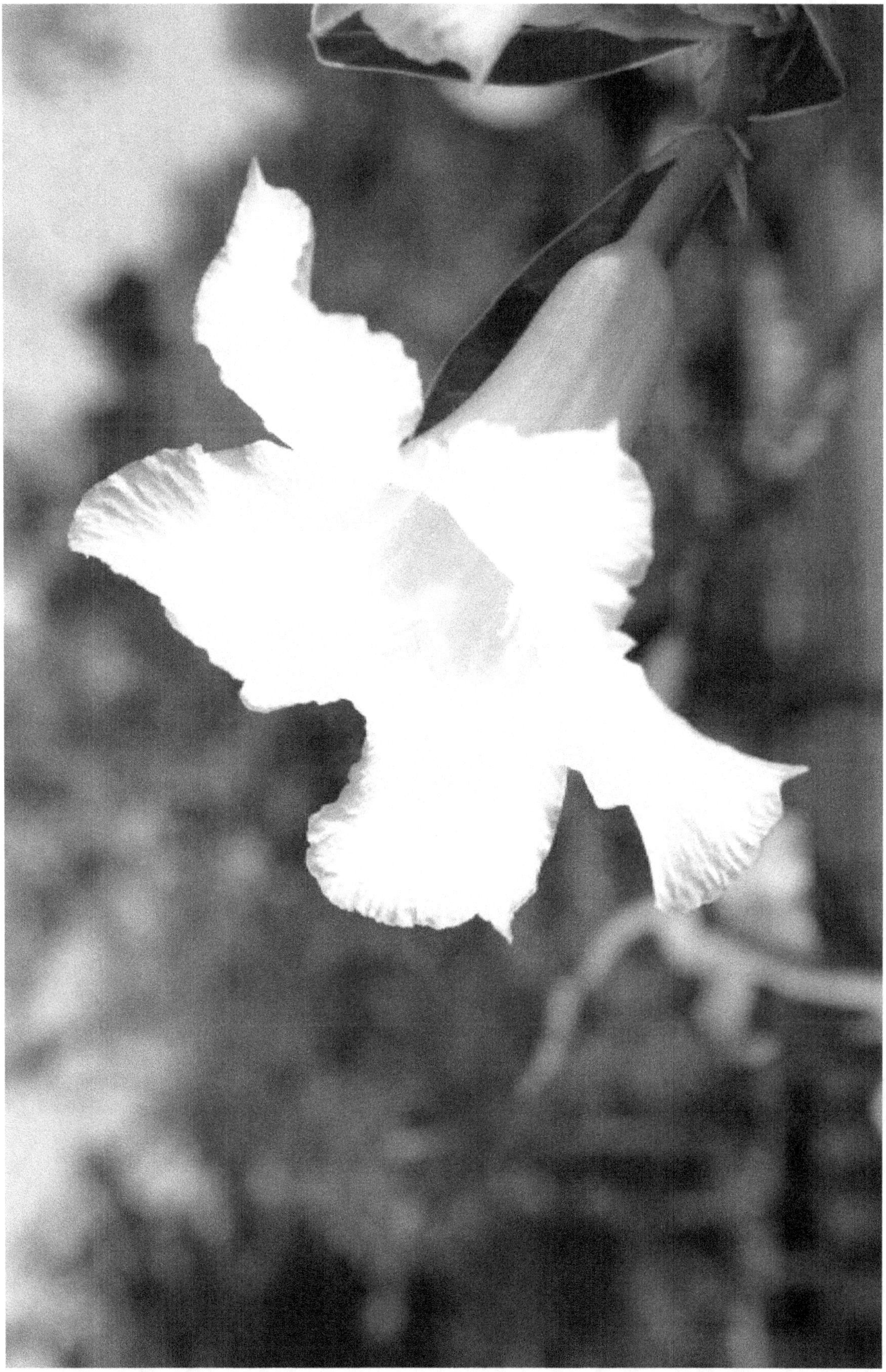

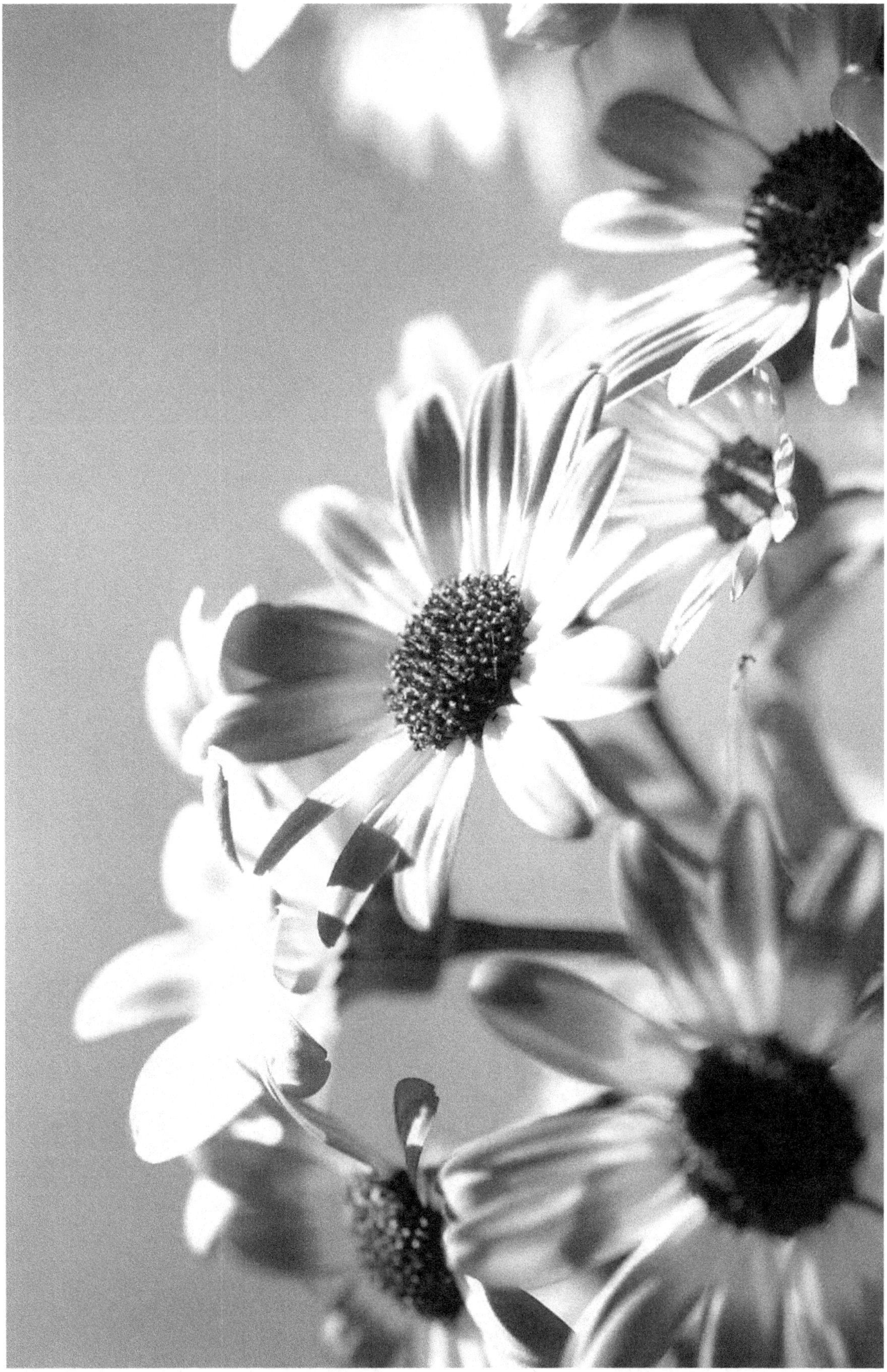

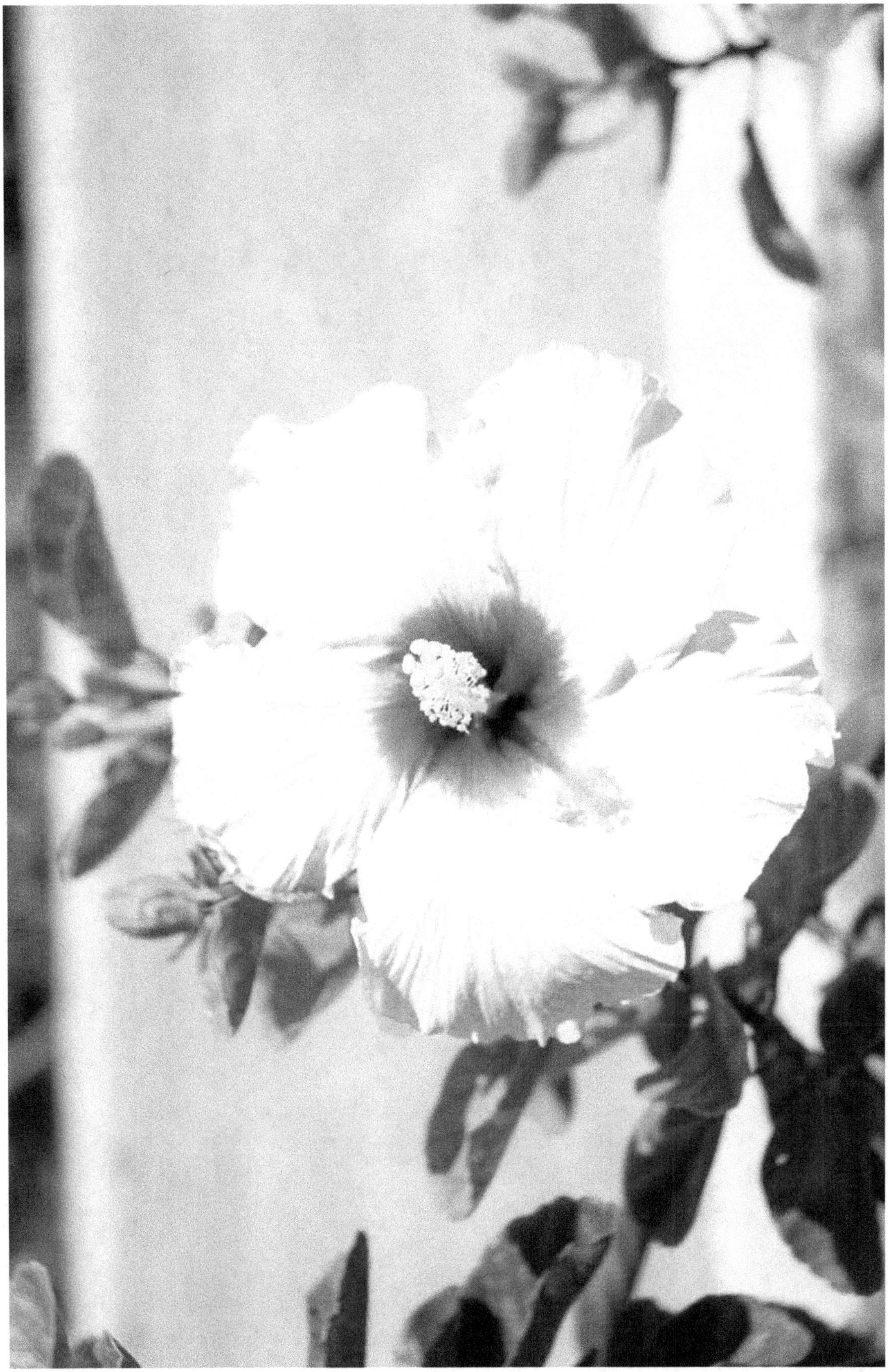

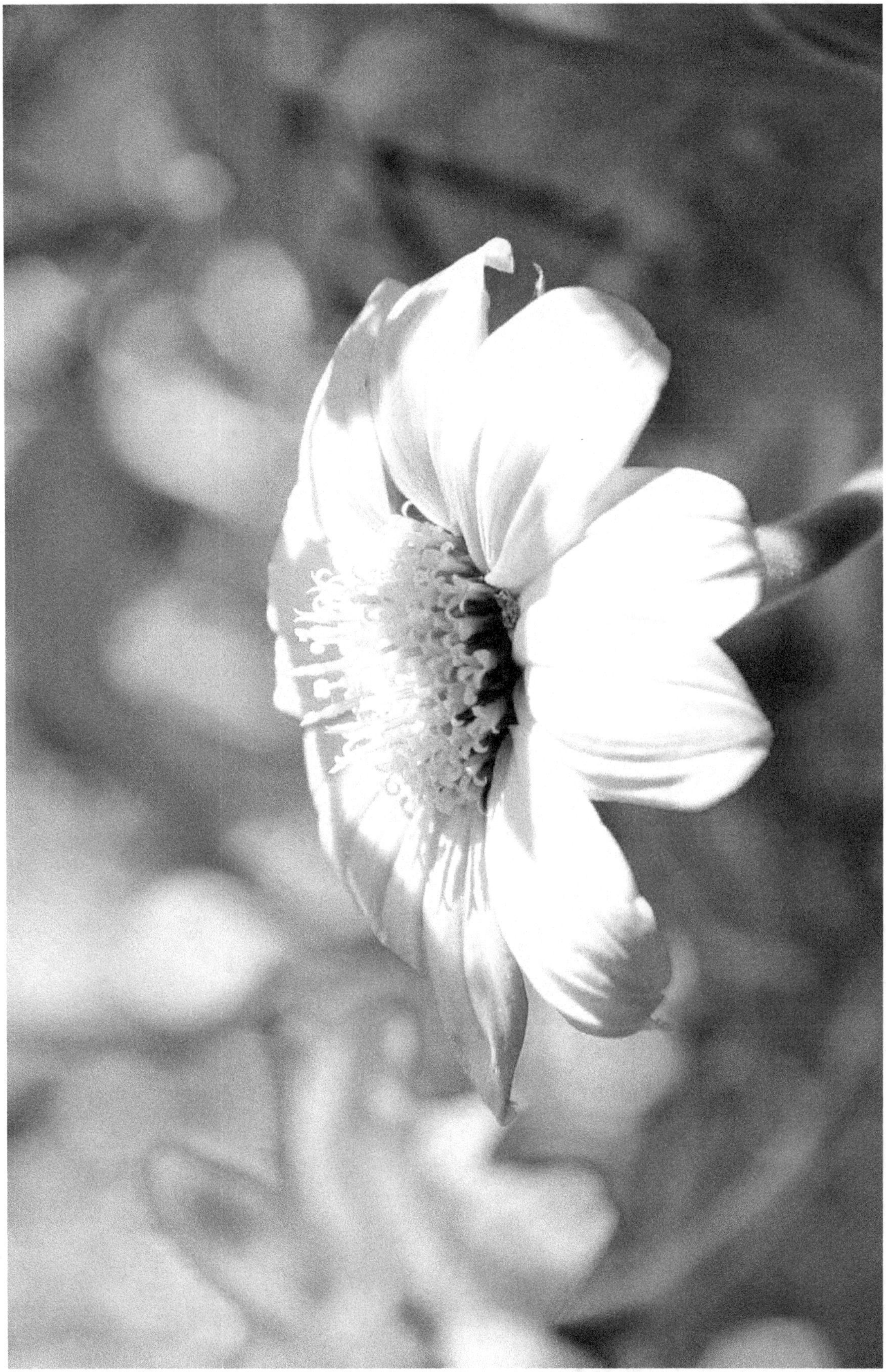

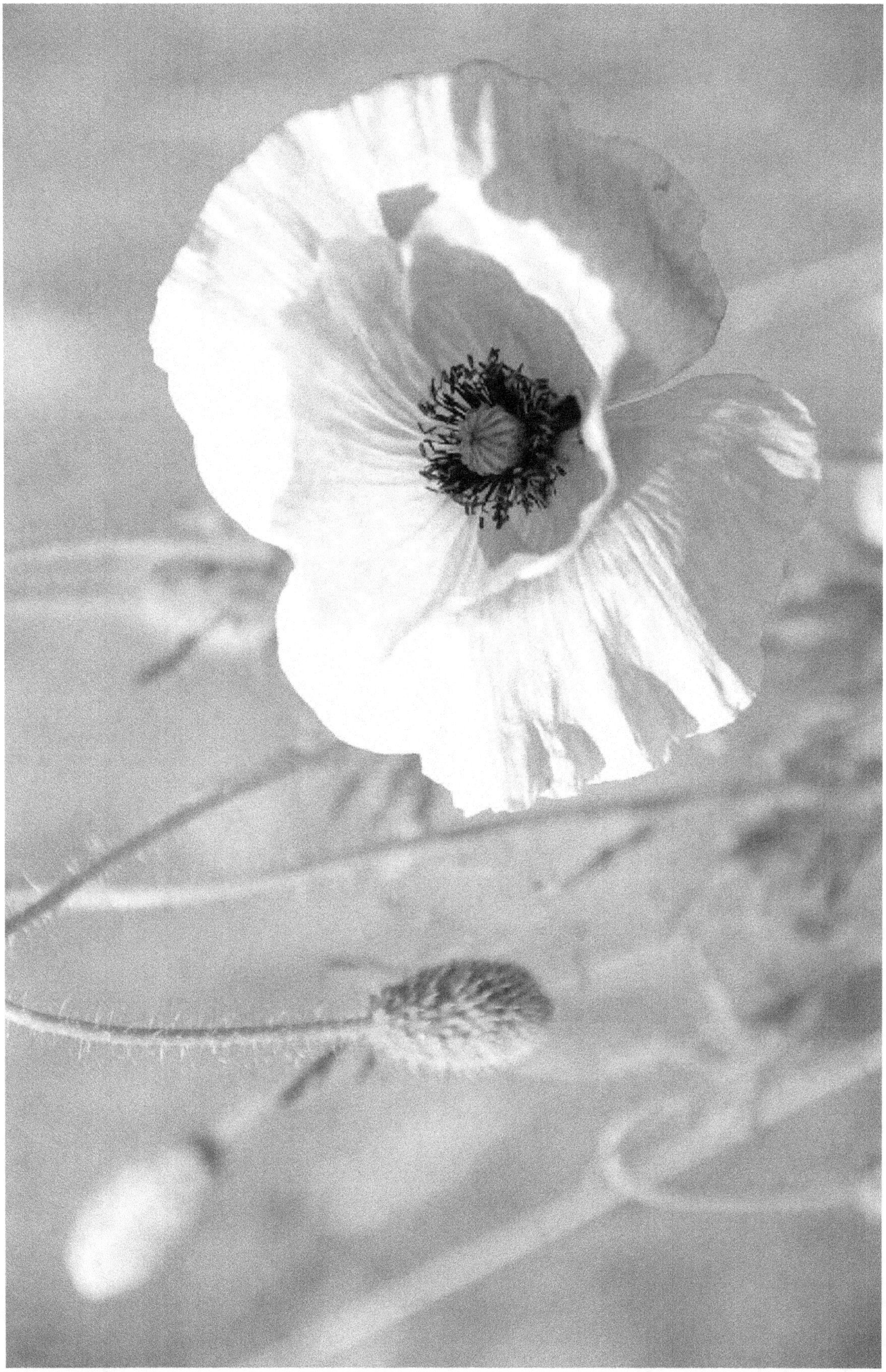

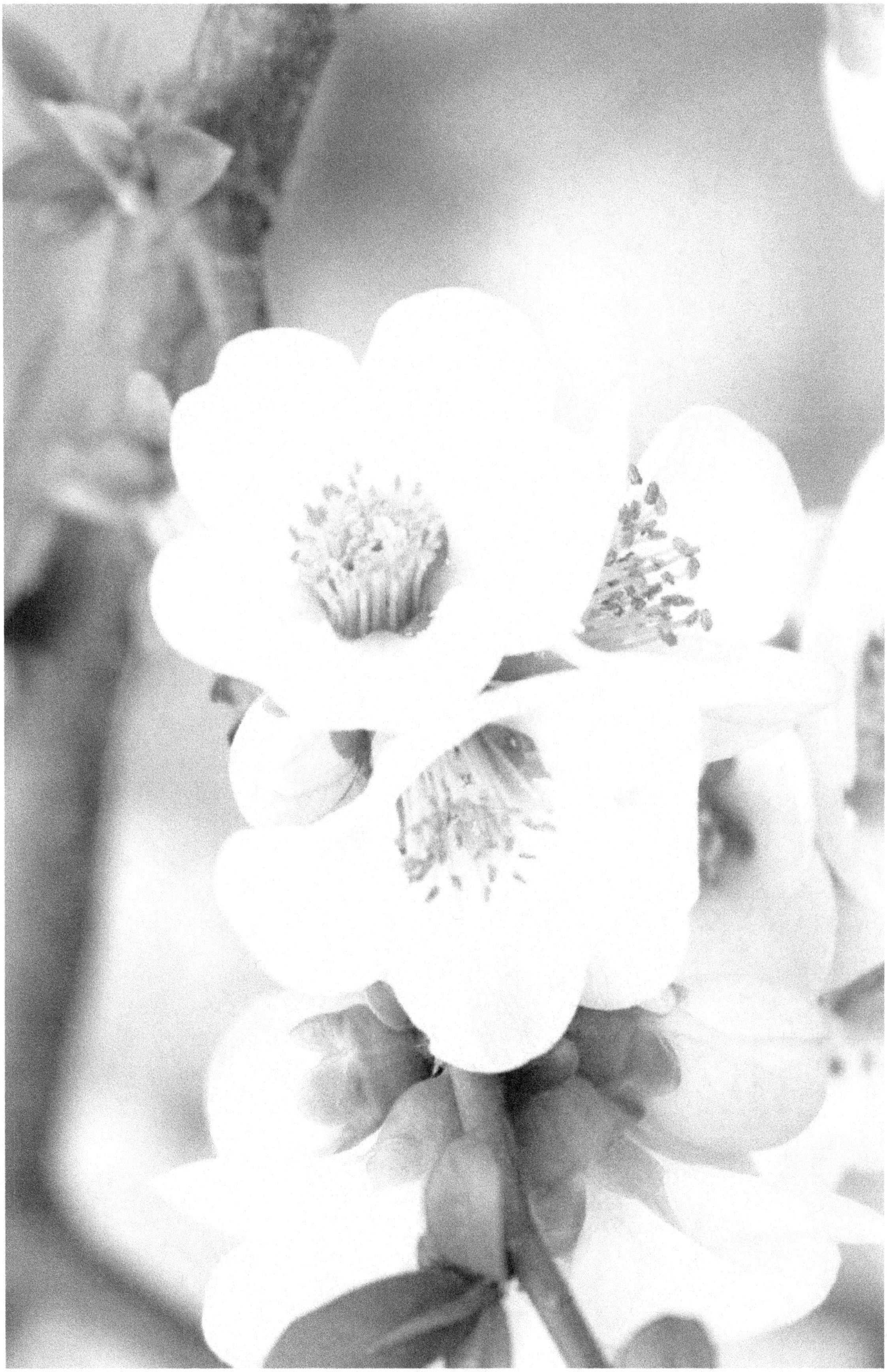

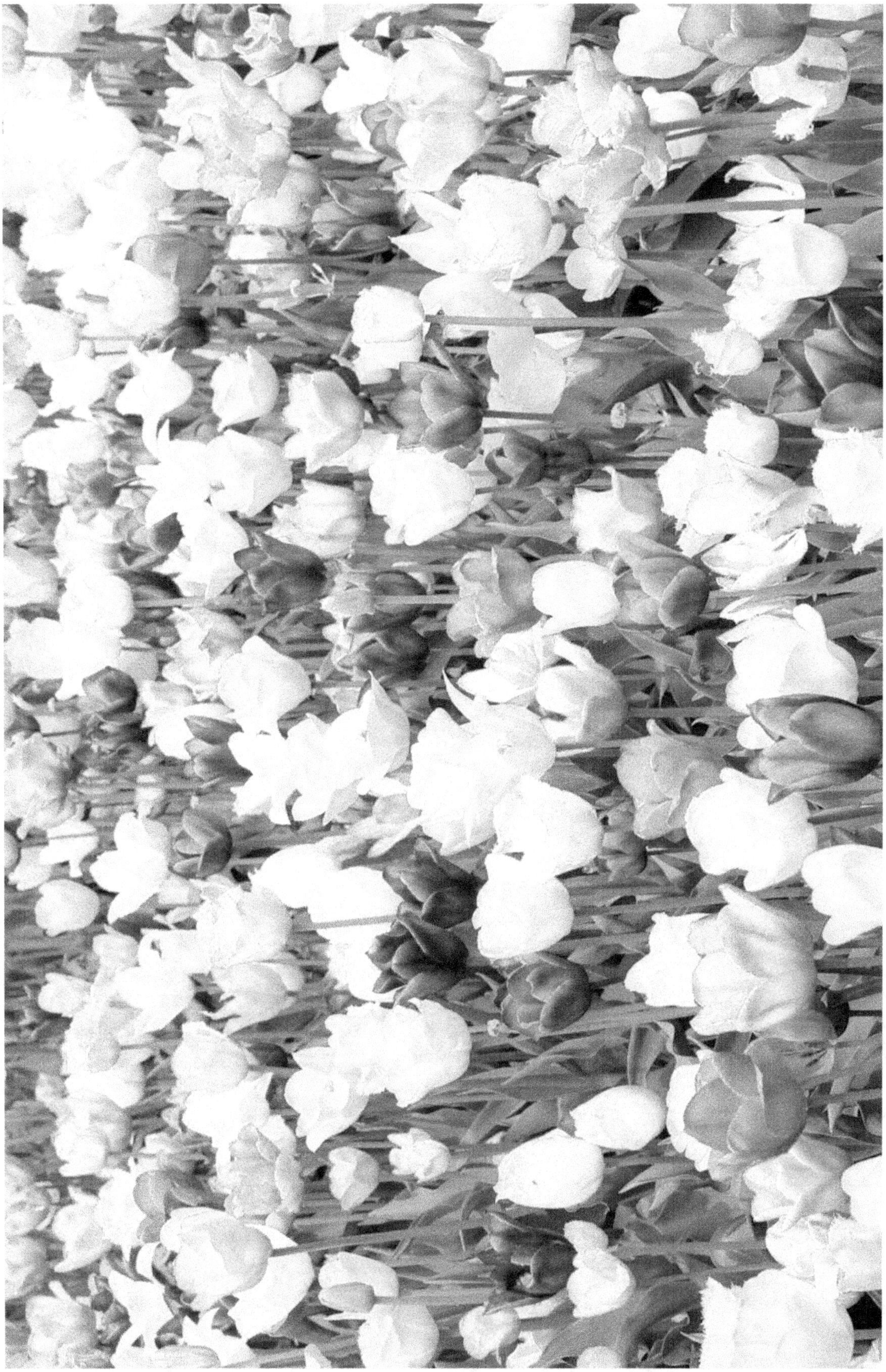

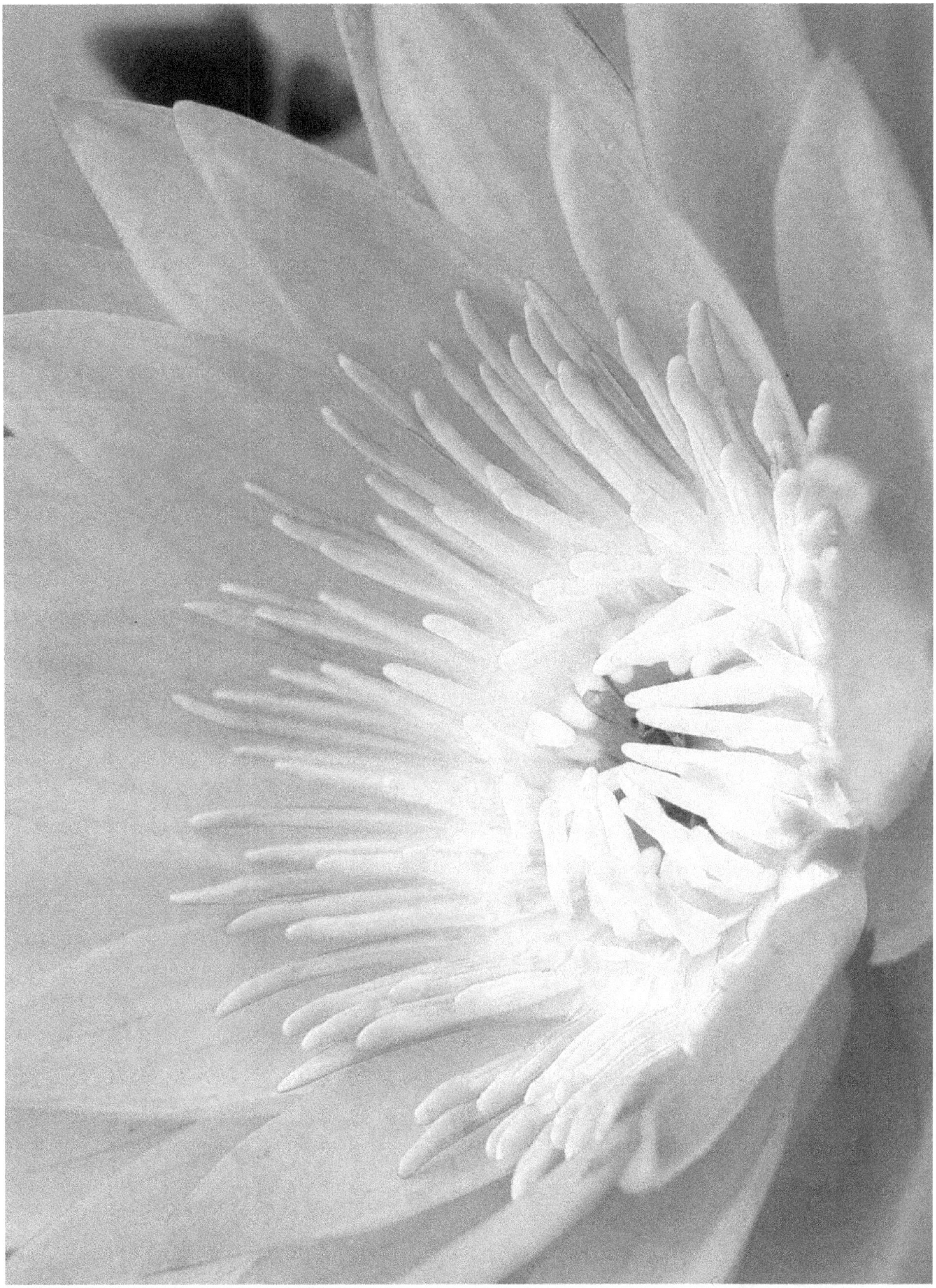

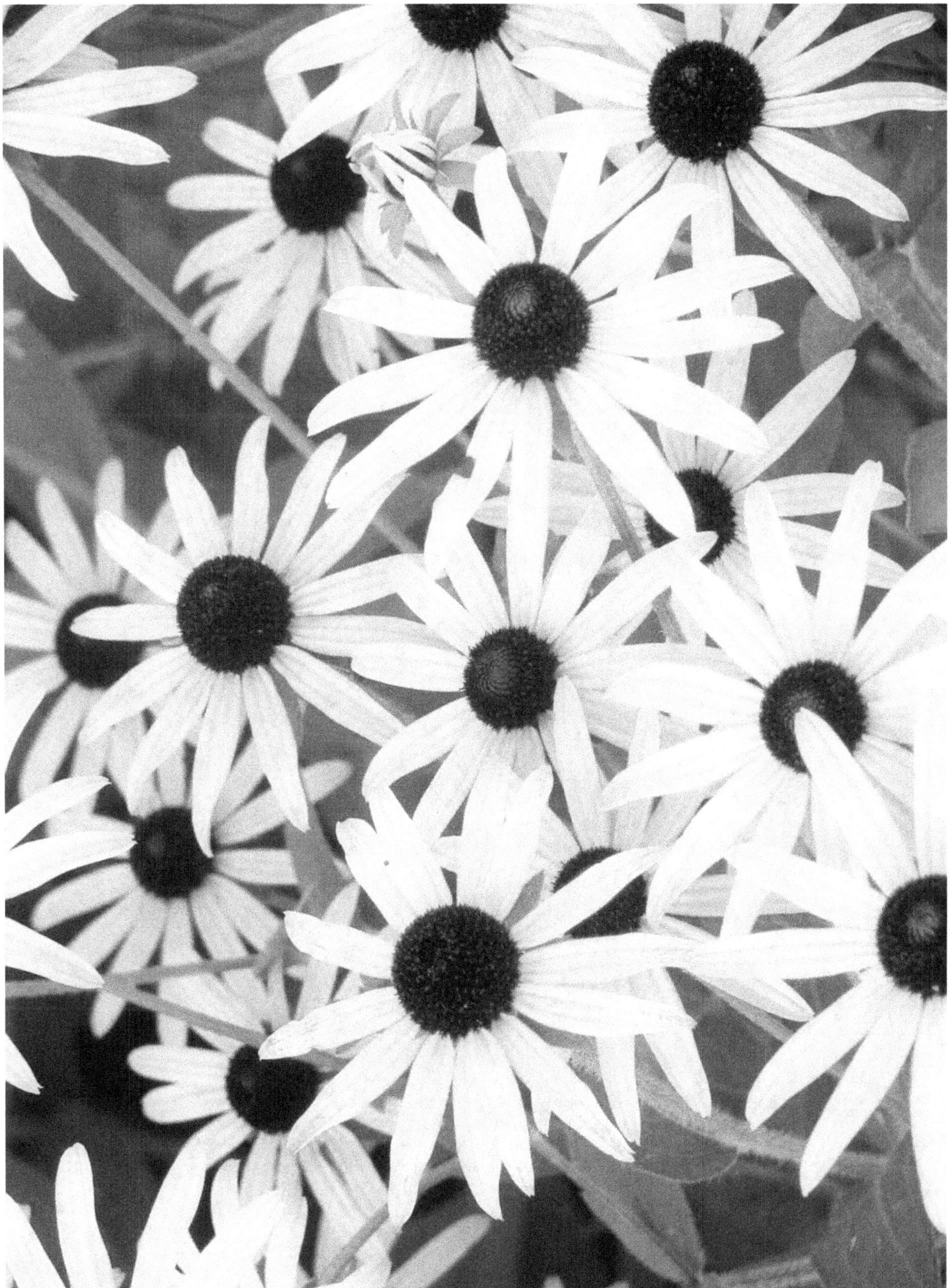

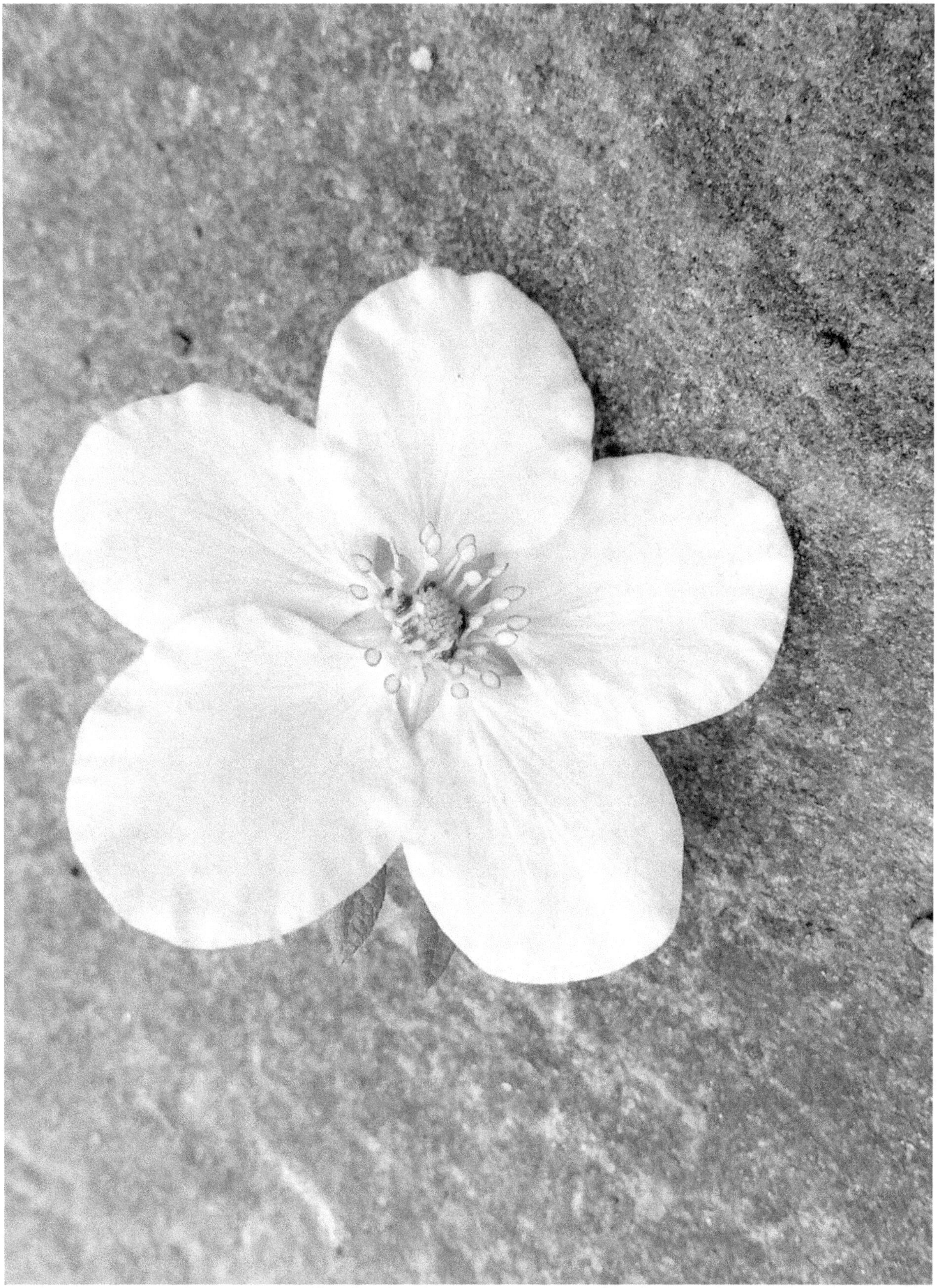

www.ingramcontent.com/pod-product-compliance
Lightning Source LLC
Chambersburg PA
CBHW081117280526
45787CB00007B/2871